# debtor's prison

# debtor's prison

## LEWIS WARSH & JULIE HARRISON

GRANARY BOOKS  NEW YORK CITY  2001

IN ASSOCIATION WITH VISUAL STUDIES WORKSHOP

Printed and bound in the United States of America on acid free paper.
Book and cover design by Julie Harrison.

Library of Congress Cataloging-in-Publication Data

Warsh, Lewis.
  Debtor's prison / Lewis Warsh & Julie Harrison.
    p.cm.
  ISBN 1-887123-58-X (pbk. : acid-free paper)
    I. Harrison, Julie. II. Title.

PS3573.A782 D4 2001
818'.5407--dc21

                                              2001040596

This book was produced in part during an artists' residency at Visual Studies Workshop,
funded by a New Technology Initiative from the New York State Council on the Arts.

Granary Books, Inc.
307 Seventh Avenue, Suite 1401
New York, NY 10001 USA
www.granarybooks.com

Visual Studies Workshop
31 Prince Street
Rochester, NY 14607
www.vsw.org

Distributed to the trade by D.A.P./Distributed Art Publishers
155 Avenue of the Americas, Second Floor
New York, NY 10013-1507
Orders: (800) 338-BOOK
Tel.: (212) 627-1999    Fax: (212) 627-9484

Also available from Small Press Distribution
1341 Seventh Street
Berkeley, CA 94710
Orders: (800) 869-7553
Tel.: (510) 524-1668    Fax: (510) 524-0582
www.spdbooks.org

*for Steve Clay*

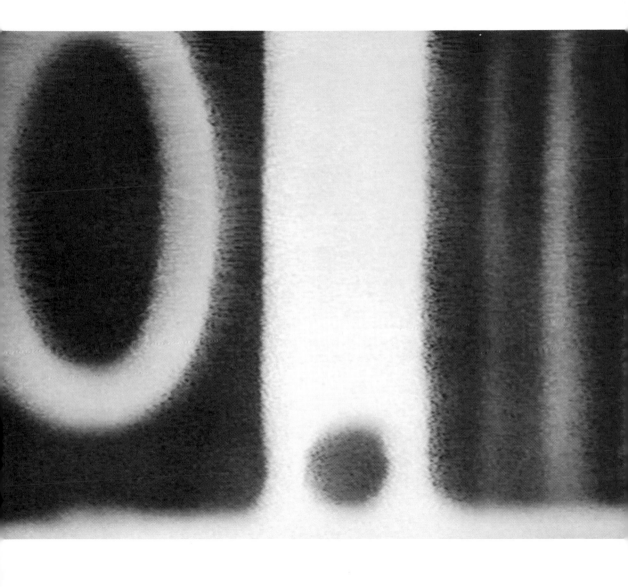

A rock carved by Michelangelo
in the form of a snake

*reflections of flora / hard of hearing*

The person beside you is breathing
in her sleep

*coerce, coerce / harass, harass*

Her thoughts are like a series of windows
covered with dust

*arable soil / mental picture*

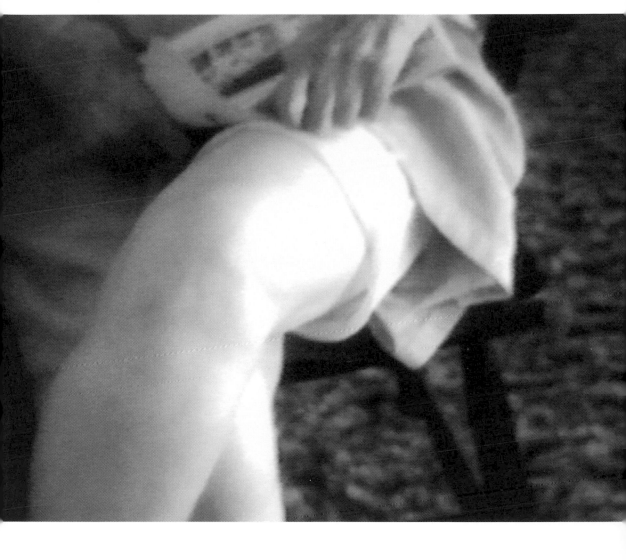

Nothing she had done before prepared her
for this moment

*ruthless creditor / passive recipient*

My head reaches up to your waist when I stand
on my toes

*lunar paraphrase / angelic thread*

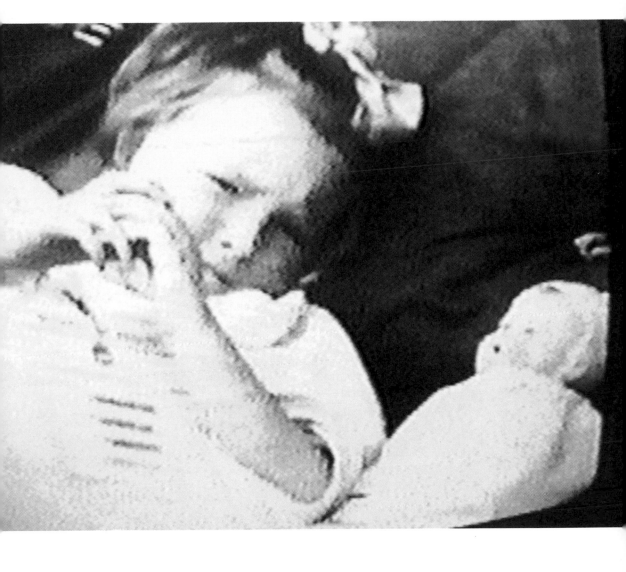

A woman in high heels beckons
from a street corner

*white wall, black hole / nothing discernible*

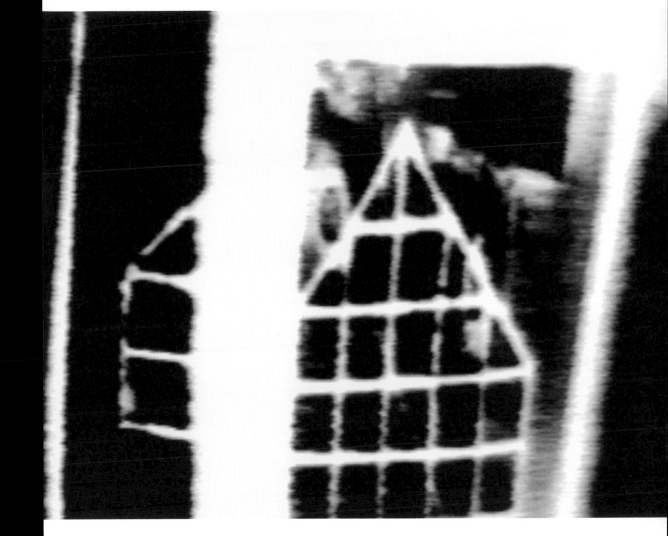

The people who stopped loving one another
were staring out the window

*zero benchmark / no one but me*

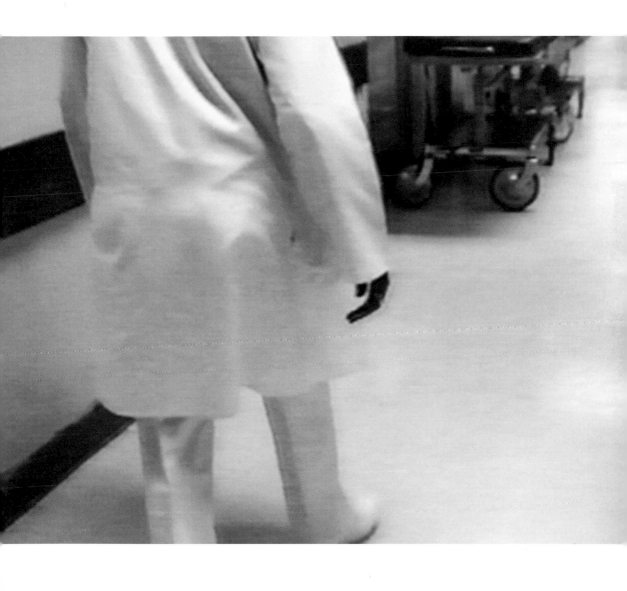

You crawled towards me naked
across the rug

*shift change at the main gate / cast of thousands*

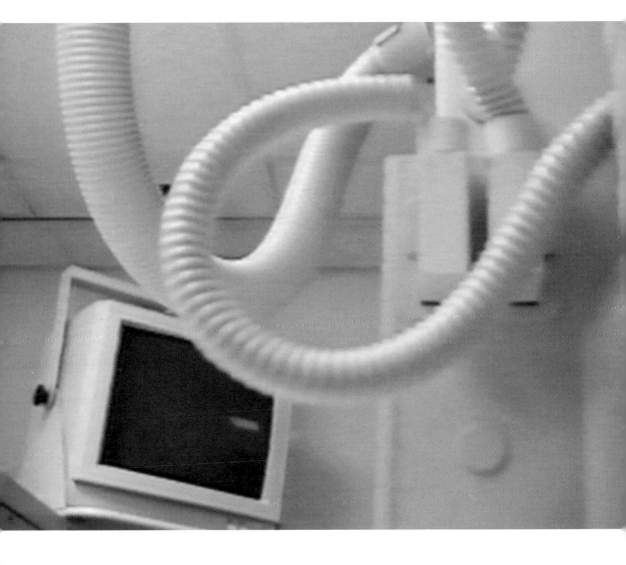

Self-discipline is necessary if you want to forget something

*no parameters / no parameters*

Attachment, detachment, cloud cover, free of pain

*my heart touches bottom / my heart touches bottom*

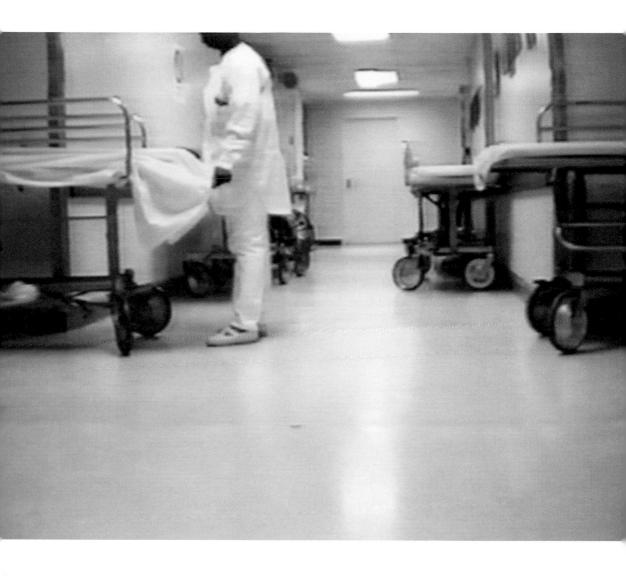

He prayed to something beautiful
that didn't have a name

*concave backdrop / luna crescent*

You, your body, the salt in the air
on my tongue

*organic connection / relevant future*

Facial blemishes, the taste of the sea
on my lips

*a dream of loneliness / round glasses with wire frames*

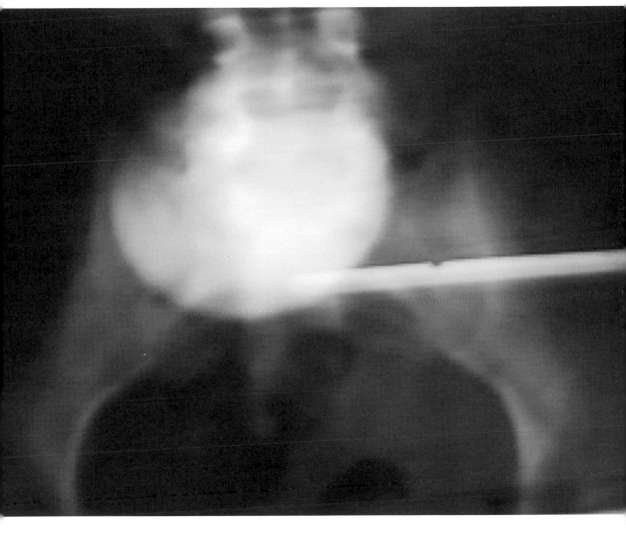

The things you say come back to you
like spoiled porridge

*paths of snow / no conviction*

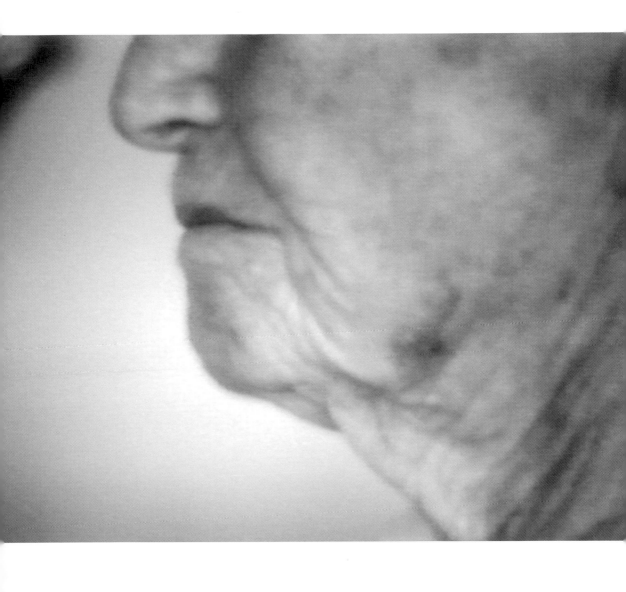

It seemed like you had never undressed
in her presence

*enmeshment of opposites / no one to blame*

In the dark, I couldn't tell whether it was her body
or his

*suspicions unwarranted / endless embrace*

A threat of eviction propels the tenants
into the street

*it smells like licorice / it smells like licorice*

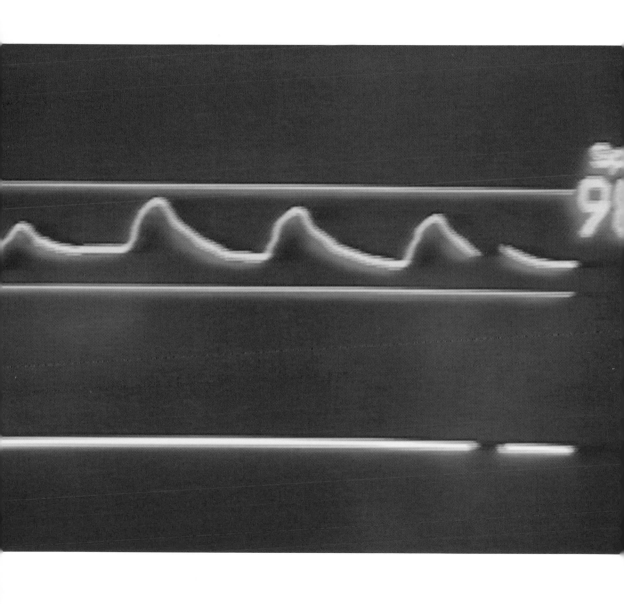

We tend to be attracted to people who look like
people we used to love

*statement of intent / human ceiling*

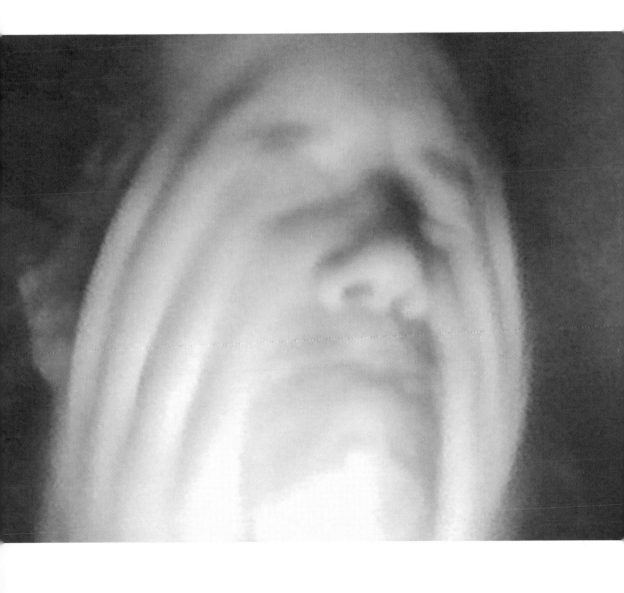

Listen to the hum of the woman behind
the beaded curtain at the end of the alley

*conscious baptism / paths of snow*

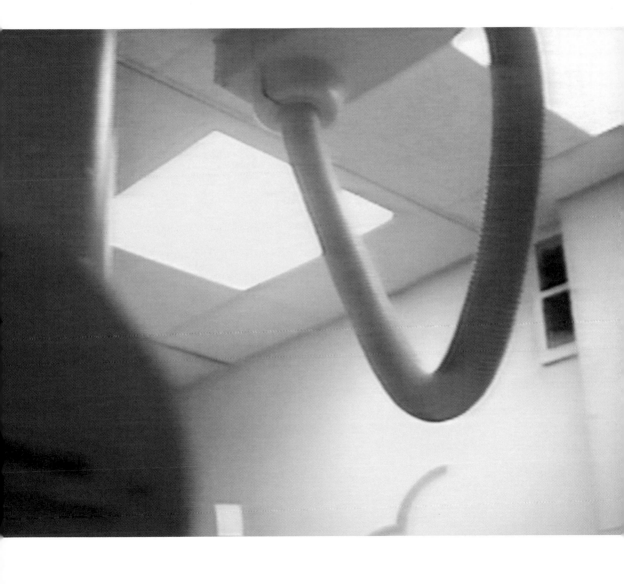

In control of nothing but writing & even writing
I'm out of control

*protective custody / screams in the night*

I knocked on the bathroom door to see
if she was still alive

*academic discourse / unleavened bread*

You who crossed the street when you saw
me coming

*blind coincidence / nothing to lose*

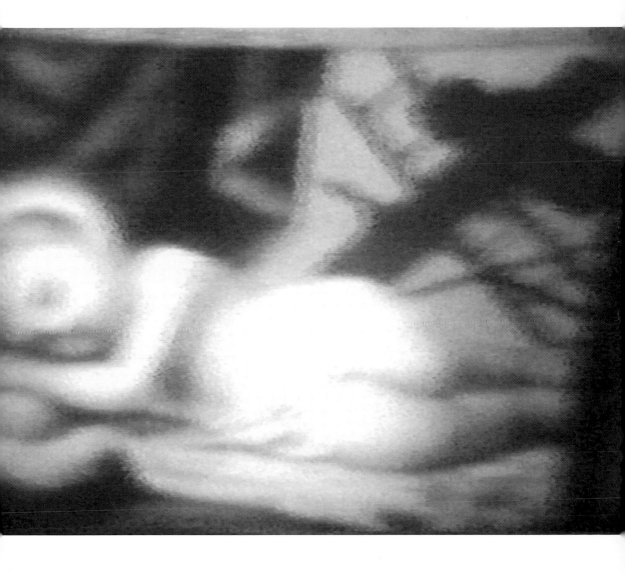

We hold on to something by not letting it out of
our memory

*coherent sequence / coherent sequence*

Every new person is a messenger, but the
message is open to question

*the warranty has expired / the warranty has expired*

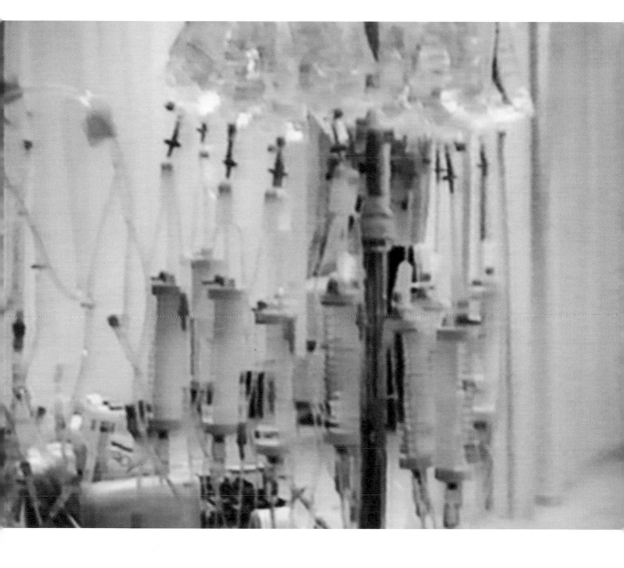

I call the waitress to bring us
our check

*manicure, manicure / interference, interference*

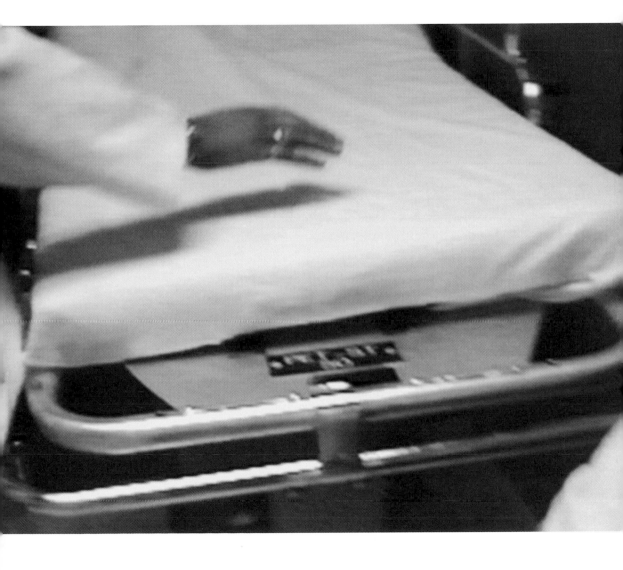

She listens to what you say
& responds accordingly

*dangerous propensity / no one to blame*

The men's room, a parking lot, her face
in the rear-view mirror

*negative dependency / start over & tell the truth*

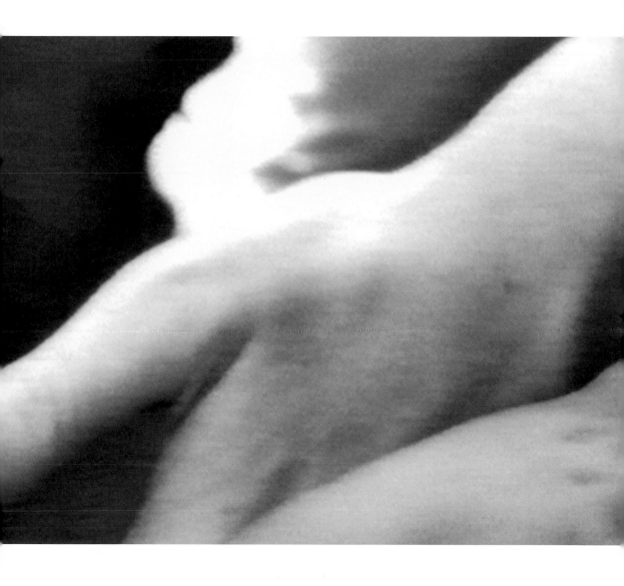

He locked the door of the castle
& threw away the key

*dusty carapace / the wrong end of the spectrum*

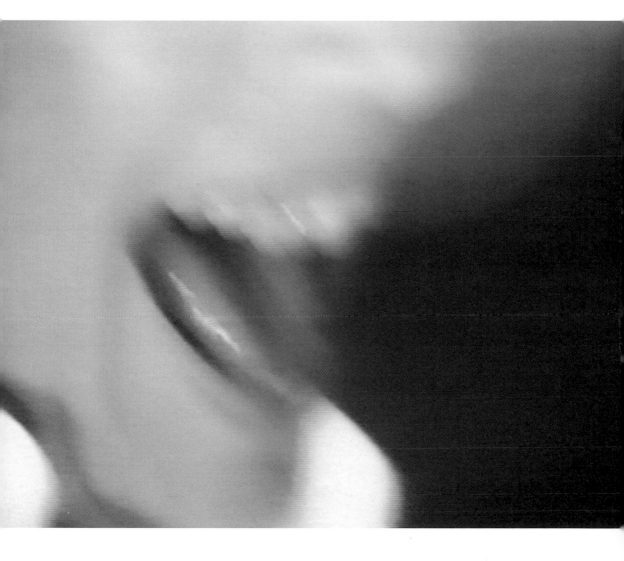

The leading lady was poisoned by
her understudy

girlish harmonies / puzzled stars

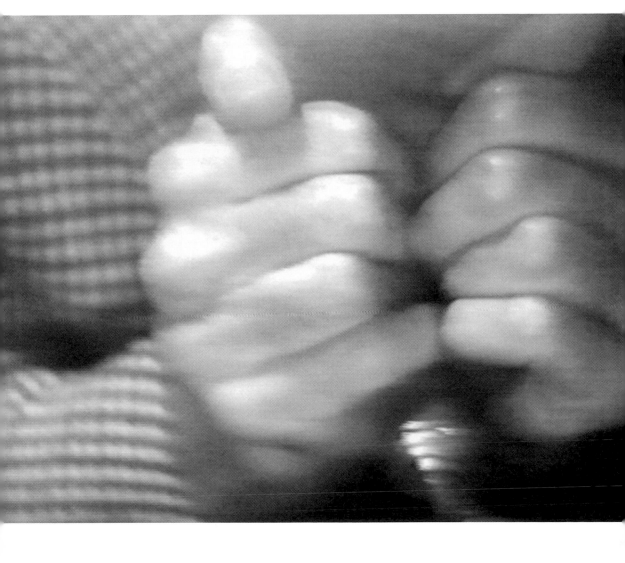

Empty hangers in the closet, the world
keeps spinning

*Yes for happiness / No for truth*

A person I never saw before calling
my name

*displaced accent / reliable buffer*

Jealousy & possessiveness are things
of the past

*biblical exegesis / indecipherable memory*

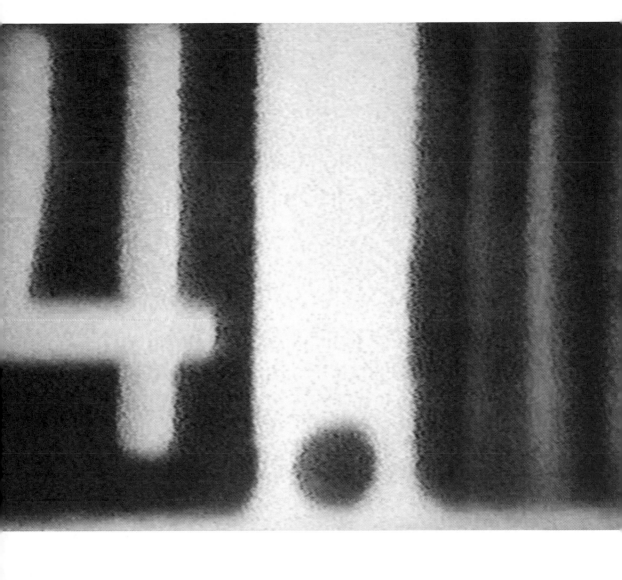

A list of samples drops like wax
from the tip of my thumb

*profit equals loss / ruthless creditor*

A tiny speedboat bouncing over choppy
waves

*brightness of yearning / a rivulet at the curb's edge*

Another person is always responding
to what you say

*debtor's prison / debtor's prison*

A long way from exactitude, but hard
of hearing

*eat without swallowing / nothing to lose*

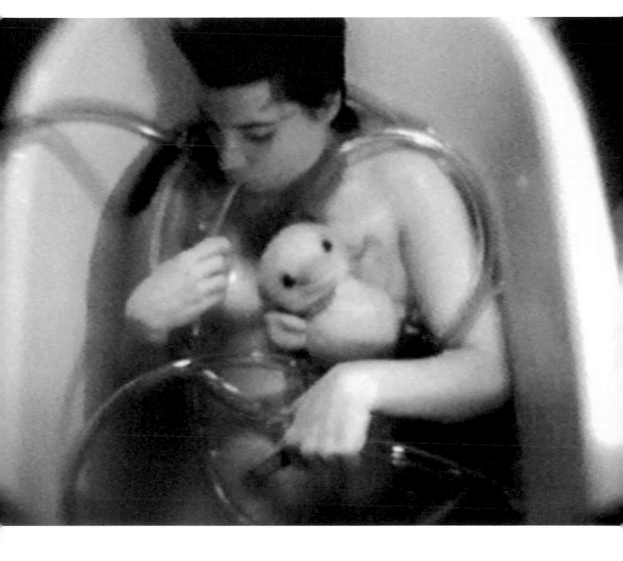

Listen to the scratchy record of the men
smoking in the alley

*footnote to Plato / blind conviction*

If you ask me nicely I'll tell you
the truth

*"still" as in "still life" / an animal like me*

The word is still the thing, we must
go on weeping

*nasty customer / nasty customer*

The weather lady caved in to pressure
to remove her dress

*passing reference / passing reference*

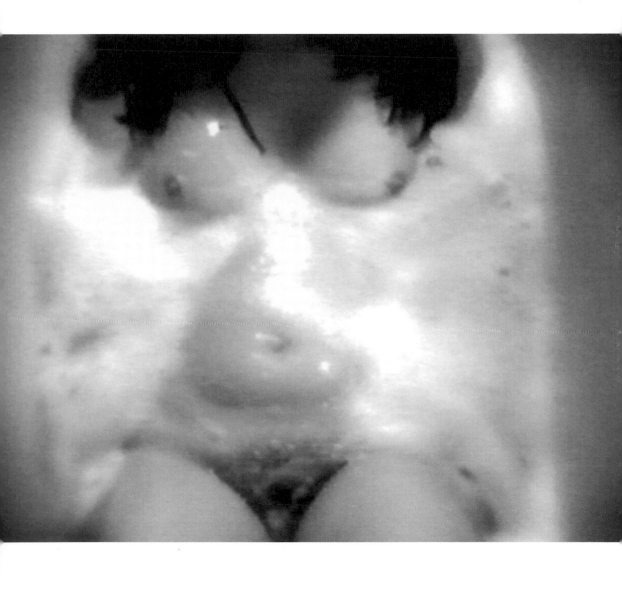

Listen to the sound of the snow falling
on the debris in the alley

*inaugural sunrise / inaugural sunrise*

An usher leads us down the aisle
with a flashlight

*displaced accent / furtive gaze*

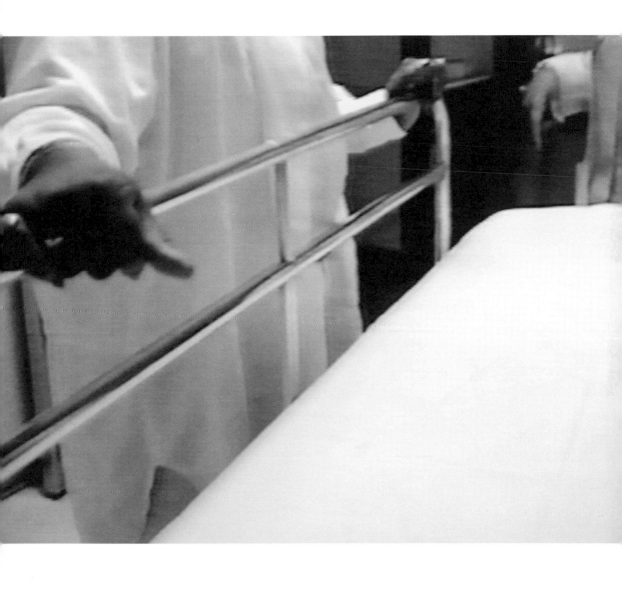

I was thinking of you, in a different context, I said
your name in my sleep

*no questions asked / no questions asked*

I hid my head in the muddy ground
but no one noticed

*redwood barstool / bouffant hairdo*

Backed the car into a ditch when no one was
looking

*line of demarcation / nothing to lose*

It's possible to wear the same clothing
as the person who died

*dusty carapace / plaintive mourning*

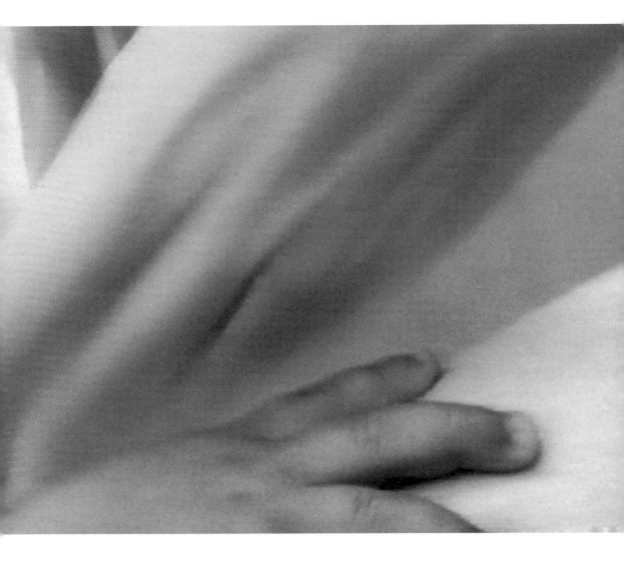

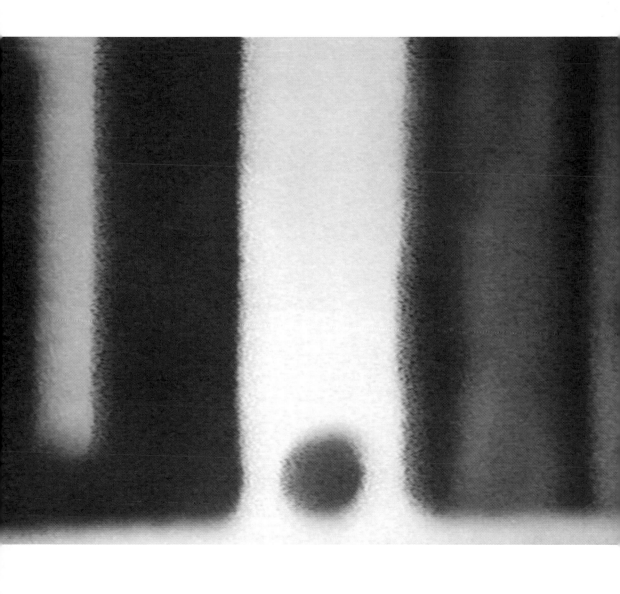

There's only one way this void can be filled
& that's by putting words on paper

*footsteps on the ceiling / swollen gland*

Perhaps there's an island in the Pacific that hasn't been invaded by our unhappiness

*voice of conscience / no longer visible*

You can read the sentence backwards & it still means
the same thing

*surgical intervention / mental picture*

I woke up with your name
on my lips

*icy precipice / icy precipice*

The expression on my face changes
depending on my mood

*elixer of immortality / essence of life*

It's almost Wednesday & I'm free of words

*solitary confinement / awkward embrace*